THE STEPS TO FREEDOM IN CHRIST

REVISED

NEIL T. ANDERSON

Gospel Light

Gospel Light is a Christian publisher dedicated to serving the local church. We believe God's vision for Gospel Light is to provide church leaders with biblical, user-friendly materials that will help them evangelize, disciple and minister to children, youth and families.

It is our prayer that this Gospel Light resource will help you discover biblical truth for your own life and help you minister to others. May God richly bless you.

For a free catalog of resources from Gospel Light, please contact your Christian supplier or contact us at 1-800-4-GOSPEL *or* www.gospellight.com.

PUBLISHING STAFF
William T. Greig, Chairman
Kyle Duncan, Publisher
Dr. Elmer L. Towns, Senior Consulting Publisher
Pam Weston, Senior Editor
Patti Pennington Virtue, Associate Editor
Jeff Kempton, Editorial Assistant
Hilary Young, Editorial Assistant
Bayard Taylor, M.Div., Senior Editor, Biblical and Theological Issues
Kevin Parks, Cover Designer
Debi Thayer, Designer

ISBN 0-8307-2878-3
© 2000, 2001 Neil T. Anderson
First edition 2000, published for the United Kingdom by Monarch Books
Second edition 2001, published by Gospel Light
All rights reserved.
Printed in the U.S.A.

CONTENTS

The Steps to Freedom in Christ   5

    Step One: Counterfeit vs. Real   8

    Step Two: Deception vs. Truth   12

    Step Three: Bitterness vs. Forgiveness   19

    Step Four: Rebellion vs. Submission   23

    Step Five: Pride vs. Humility   25

    Step Six: Bondage vs. Freedom   28

    Step Seven: Curses vs. Blessings   34

Maintaining Your Freedom   36

Appendices

    Appendix A: Evaluate Your Priorities   43

    Appendix B: Satanic Rituals or Heavy Occult Activity   45

    Appendix C: The Truth About Your Father God   47

    Appendix D: Resolving Anxiety   49

    Appendix E: Steps to Overcoming Fears   53

    Appendix F: Dealing with Prejudice and Bigotry   58

    Appendix G: Seeking the Forgiveness of Others   60

Endnotes   62

The Steps to Freedom in Christ

"It was for freedom that Christ set us free; therefore keep standing firm and do not be subject again to a yoke of slavery" (Galatians 5:1). If you have received Christ as your Savior, He has already set you free through His victory over sin and death on the cross. The question is: Are you living victoriously in Christ's freedom or are you living in bondage, however subtle or strong?

Christ offers you freedom from personal and spiritual conflicts, freedom from sin and the negative programming of your past, freedom from the damaging effects of guilt and unforgiveness. Freedom opens the pathway to knowing, loving, worshiping and obeying God. It is the joyful experience of living by faith according to what God says is true and in the power of the Holy Spirit, and it means not carrying out the desires of the flesh. It doesn't mean perfection, but it is a growing and abundant life in Christ who alone can meet our deepest need for life, identity, acceptance, security and significance.

REGAINING YOUR FREEDOM

If you are not experiencing this life of freedom, it may be because you have not stood firm in the faith or lived according to who you are in Christ. Somehow you have returned again to a yoke of slavery (see Galatians 5:1). Your eternal destiny is not at stake, but your daily victory is.

No matter how difficult your life might be, there is great news for you. You are not a helpless victim caught between two nearly equal but opposite heavenly superpowers. Satan is a liar and a deceiver, and the only way he can have power over you is if you believe his lies. Only God is omnipotent (all powerful), omnipresent (always present) and omniscient (all knowing). Sometimes the reality of sin and the presence of evil may seem more real than the presence of God, but that's part of Satan's deception. Satan is a defeated foe, and we are alive in Christ.

The Steps to Freedom in Christ do not set you free. *Who* sets you free is Christ; *what* sets you free is your response to Him in repentance and faith. The Steps provide an opportunity for you to have an encounter with God, the Wonderful Counselor, by submitting to Him and resisting the devil (see James 4:7). They are a means of resolving personal and spiritual conflicts that have kept you from experiencing the freedom and victory Christ purchased for you on the cross. Your freedom will be the result of what you choose to believe, confess, forgive, renounce and forsake. No one can do that for you.

THE BATTLE FOR YOUR MIND

There is a battle going on for your mind—the control center of all that you think and do. The opposing thoughts you may experience as you go through these steps can affect you only if you believe them. You may have nagging thoughts such as, *This isn't going to work* or *God doesn't love me.* Don't believe Satan's deceptions; don't pay any attention to accusing or threatening thoughts.

The battle for your mind can only be won as you personally choose truth. As you go through the process, remember that Satan is under no obligation to obey your thoughts. Only God has complete knowledge of your mind, because He alone is omniscient (all knowing). Find a private place where you can verbally process each step. You can submit to God inwardly, but you need to resist the devil by reading aloud each prayer and in that way verbally renounce, forgive, confess, etc.

These Steps address critical issues between you and God. You probably will find it possible to process them on your own because Jesus is the Wonderful Counselor. However, some people do feel they need additional help. If you experience difficulty, ask your pastor or a counselor or someone familiar with the Steps to help you.

Both gaining and maintaining your freedom will be greatly enhanced if you first read *Victory over the Darkness* and *The Bondage Breaker.* They will help you further understand the reality of the spiritual world and your relationship to it. While these Steps can play a major role in your continuing process of discipleship, there is no such thing as instant maturity. Renewing your mind and conforming to the image of God is a lifelong process.

Regardless of the source of any difficulty you may have, you have nothing to lose and possibly everything to gain by praying through these issues. If your problems stem from a source other than those covered in these Steps, you may need to seek professional help. The real focus here is your relationship with God. The lack of resolution of any one of these issues will affect your intimacy with Him and your daily victory in Christ.

TRUST GOD TO LEAD YOU

Each Step is explained so you will have no problem knowing what to do. It doesn't make any difference whether or not there are evil spirits present; God is always present. If you experience any resistance, stop and pray. If you experience some mental opposition, just ignore it. It is just a thought, and it can have no power over you unless you believe it. Throughout the process, you will be asking God to lead you. He is the One who grants repentance leading to a knowledge of the truth that sets you free (see 2 Timothy 2:24-26). Begin the Steps with the following prayer and declaration. (It is not necessary to read the words in the parentheses; they are there for clarification or reference.)

May the Lord bless and guide you as you go through these Steps. Then, having found your freedom in Christ, you can help others experience the joy of their salvation.

PRAYER

Dear Heavenly Father,

I acknowledge Your presence in this room and in my life. You are the only omniscient (all knowing), omnipotent (all powerful) and omnipresent (always present) God. I am dependent upon You, for apart from You I can do nothing. I stand in the truth that all authority in heaven and on Earth has been given to the resurrected Christ, and because I am in Christ, I share that authority in order to make disciples and set captives free. I ask You to fill me with Your Holy Spirit and lead me into all truth. I pray for Your complete protection and ask for Your guidance. In Jesus' name, amen.

DECLARATION

In the name and authority of the Lord Jesus Christ, I command Satan and all evil spirits to release me in order that I can be free to know and to choose to do the will of God. As a child of God who is seated with Christ in the heavenlies, I command every evil spirit to leave my presence. I belong to God and the evil one cannot touch me.

COUNTERFEIT VS. REAL

The first step toward experiencing your freedom in Christ is to renounce (verbally reject) all past or present involvement with occult practices, cult teachings and rituals, and non-Christian religions.

You must renounce any activity or group which denies Jesus Christ or offers guidance through any source other than the absolute authority of the Bible. Any group that requires dark or secret initiations, ceremonies, promises or pacts should also be renounced. Begin this step by praying aloud:

> **Dear Heavenly Father,**
> **I ask You to bring to my mind anything and everything that I have done knowingly or unknowingly that involves occult, cult or non-Christian teachings or practices. I want to experience Your freedom by renouncing all counterfeit teachings and practices. In Jesus' name, amen.**

Even if you took part in something and thought it was just a game or a joke, you need to renounce it. Satan will try to take advantage of anything he can in our lives, so it is always wise to be as thorough as possible. Even if you were just standing by and watching others do it, you need to renounce your passive involvement. You may not have even realized at the time that what was going on was evil. Still, go ahead and renounce it.

If something comes to your mind and you are not sure what to do about it, trust that the Spirit of God is answering your prayer, and renounce it.

The following Non-Christian Spiritual Checklist covers many of the more common occultic, cultic and non-Christian religious groups and practices. It is not a complete list, however. Feel free to add others that you were personally involved with.

After the checklist, there are some additional questions designed to help you become aware of other things you may need to renounce. Below those questions is a short prayer of confession and renunciation. Pray it aloud, filling in the blanks with the groups, teachings or practices that the Holy Spirit has prompted you to renounce during this time of personal evaluation.

NON-CHRISTIAN SPIRITUAL CHECKLIST
(Check all those that you have participated in.)

OCCULT

- ❑ Out-of-body experience (astral projection)
- ❑ Ouija board
- ❑ Bloody Mary
- ❑ Light as a feather (or other occult games)
- ❑ Magic Eight Ball
- ❑ Spells or curses
- ❑ Mental telepathy or mental control of others
- ❑ Automatic writing
- ❑ Trances
- ❑ Spirit guides
- ❑ Fortune-telling/ divination (e.g., tea leaves)
- ❑ Tarot cards
- ❑ Levitation
- ❑ Magic—The Gathering
- ❑ Witchcraft/sorcery
- ❑ Satanism
- ❑ Palm reading
- ❑ Astrology/ horoscopes
- ❑ Hypnosis
- ❑ Seances
- ❑ Black or white magic
- ☑ Fantasy games with occult images ?

- ❑ Blood pacts or cutting yourself on purpose
- ❑ Objects of worship/ crystals/good luck charms
- ❑ Sexual spirits
- ❑ Martial arts (mysticism/ devotion to sensei)
- ❑ Superstitions
- ❑ Occult or violent video and computer games

OTHER RELIGIONS

- ❑ Buddhism (including Zen)
- ❑ Hinduism
- ❑ Islam
- ❑ Black Muslim
- ❑ Native American spirit worship
- ❑ Yoga
- ❑ Hare Krishna
- ❑ Silva Mind Control
- ❑ Bahai faith
- ❑ Rosicrucianism
- ❑ Other non-Christian religions or cults

CULTS

- ❑ Mormonism (Latter-day Saints)
- ❑ Jehovah's Witnesses (Watchtower)
- ❑ New Age (books, objects, seminars, medicine)
- ❑ Masons
- ❑ Christian Science
- ❑ Mind Science cults
- ❑ The Way International
- ❑ Unification Church (Moonies)
- ❑ The Forum (est)
- ❑ Church of the Living Word
- ❑ Children of God (Children of Love)
- ❑ Church of Scientology
- ❑ Unitarianism/ Universalism
- ❑ Transcendental meditation (TM)

List movies, TV shows, music, books, magazines or comics that the Lord is bringing to your mind (especially those that glorified Satan, caused fear or nightmares, were gruesomely violent or stimulated the flesh).

The following questions are designed to help you become aware of other things you may need to renounce.

1. Have you ever seen, heard or felt a spiritual being in your room?

2. Do you have recurring nightmares? Specifically renounce any accompanying fear.

3. Do you now have, or have you ever had, an imaginary friend, spirit guide or angel offering you guidance or companionship? If it has a name, renounce it by name.

4. Have you ever heard voices in your head or had repeating, nagging thoughts such as, *I'm dumb*, *I'm ugly*, *Nobody loves me* or *I can't do anything right*? List any specific nagging thoughts.

5. Have you ever consulted a medium, spiritist or channeler?

6. Have you ever seen or been contacted by beings you thought were aliens?

7. Have you ever made a secret vow or pact (or inner vow, e.g., *I will never . . .*)?

8. Have you ever been involved in a satanic ritual of any kind or attended a concert in which Satan was the focus?

9. What other spiritual experiences have you had that were evil, confusing or frightening? List them on a sheet of paper.

Once you have completed your checklist and the questions, confess and renounce each item you were involved in by praying the following prayer aloud:

Lord,
    I confess that I have participated in _____,
and I renounce ___ _____. Thank You that
in Christ I am forgiven.

When you have finished confessing and renouncing each item, pray the following prayer:

Lord,
    I confess that I have participated in these wrongful practices. I know they were evil and offensive in Your sight. Thank You for Your forgiveness. I renounce any and all involvement in these wrongful practices, and I choose to believe that Satan no longer has any rightful place in my life because of those involvements. In Jesus' name, amen.

EVALUATE YOUR PRIORITIES

Our priorities reveal what is important to us. These priorities don't necessarily have to be evil in nature to usurp God's rightful place in our lives and thus become a false god or idol. Evaluating your priorities can help you recognize where your true allegiance is, and, if necessary, restore God's rightful place in your life. (See appendix A, p. 43.)

SATANIC RITUALS OR HEAVY OCCULT ACTIVITY

There are special renunciations for anyone who either has or suspects that they might have had a deeper exposure to satanism. They provide an opportunity for you to verbally renounce any involvement (voluntary or involuntary) in the Kingdom of Darkness and then affirm your position in the Kingdom of Light. If you have experienced heavy involvement in the occult or think you may have been exposed to it, it is important to have an experienced friend, pastor or counselor guide you through these special renunciations. (See appendix B, p. 45.)

STEP 2

DECEPTION VS. TRUTH

God's Word is true, and we need to accept His truth in the innermost part of our being (see Psalm 51:6). Whether or not we feel it is true, we need to believe it is true! Jesus is the truth, the Holy Spirit is the Spirit of truth, the Word of God is truth and we are admonished to speak the truth in love (see John 14:6; 16:13; 17:17; Ephesians 4:15).

The believer in Christ has no business deceiving others by lying, telling white lies, exaggerating, stretching the truth, or anything relating to falsehoods. Satan is the father of lies and he seeks to keep people in bondage through deception. It is the truth in Jesus that sets us free (see John 8:32-36,44; 2 Timothy 2:26; Revelation 12:9). We will find real joy and freedom when we stop living a lie and live openly in the truth. After confessing his sin, King David wrote, "How blessed [happy] is the man . . . in whose spirit there is no deceit!" (Psalm 32:2).

We have been called to walk in the light (see 1 John 1:7). When we are sure God loves and accepts us, we can be free to own up to our sins and face reality, instead of running and hiding from the truth and painful circumstances.

Start this step by praying the following prayer aloud. Don't let any threatening, opposing thoughts, such as, *This is a waste of time* or *I wish I could believe this, but I just can't,* keep you from praying and choosing the truth. Even if this is difficult for you, work your way through this step. God will strengthen you as you rely on Him.

> Dear Heavenly Father,
>
> I know that You want me to know the truth, believe the truth, speak the truth and live in accordance with the truth. Thank You that it is the truth that will set me free. In many ways I have been deceived by Satan, the father of lies, and I have deceived myself as well.
>
> Father, I pray in the name of the Lord Jesus Christ, by virtue of His shed blood and Resurrection, asking You to rebuke all evil spirits that are deceiving me.
>
> I have trusted in Jesus alone to save me, and so I am Your forgiven child. Therefore, since You accept me just as I am in Christ, I can be free to face my sin and not try to hide. I ask for the Holy Spirit to guide me into all truth. I ask You to "search me, O God, and know my heart; try me and know my anxious thoughts; and see if there be any hurtful way in me,

and lead me in the everlasting way."[1] In the name of Jesus,
who is *the* truth, amen.

There are many ways in which Satan, the god of this world, seeks to
deceive us. Just as he did with Eve, the devil tries to convince us to rely on
ourselves and to try to get our needs met through the world around us, rather
than trusting in the provision of our Father in heaven.

The following exercise will help you discover ways you may have been
deceived. Check each area of deception that the Lord brings to your mind and
confess it, using the prayer following the list.

WAYS YOU CAN BE DECEIVED BY THE WORLD

- ☑ Believing that acquiring money and things will bring lasting happiness (see Matthew 13:22; 1 Timothy 6:10)
- ❏ Believing that excessive food and alcohol can relieve my stress and make me happy (see Proverbs 20:1; 23:19-21)
- ☑ Believing that an attractive body and personality will get me what I want (see Proverbs 31:30; 1 Peter 3:3,4)
- ☑ Believing that gratifying sexual lust will bring lasting satisfaction (see Ephesians 4:22; 1 Peter 2:11)
- ☑ Believing that I can sin without any negative consequences (see Hebrews 3:12,13)
- ☑ Believing that I need more than what God has given me in Christ (see 2 Corinthians 11:2-4,13-15)
- ❏ Believing that I can do whatever I want and no one can touch me (see Proverbs 16:18; Obadiah 3; 1 Peter 5:5)
- ❏ Believing that unrighteous people who refuse to accept Christ go to heaven anyway (see 1 Corinthians 6:9-11)
- ❏ Believing that I can associate with bad company and not become corrupted (see 1 Corinthians 15:33,34)
- ☑ Believing that I can read, see or listen to anything and not be corrupted (see Proverbs 4:23-27; 6:27,28; Matthew 5:28)
- ☑ Believing that there are no consequences on earth for my sin (see Galatians 6:7,8)
- ☑ Believing that I must gain the approval of certain people in order to be happy (see Galatians 1:10)
- ❏ Believing that I must measure up to certain standards in order to feel good about myself (see Galatians 3:2,3; 5:1)

> Lord, I confess that I have been deceived by
> _____. I thank You for Your forgiveness,
> and I commit myself to believing only Your truth. In Jesus'
> name, amen.

It is important to know that in addition to being deceived by the world, false teachers and deceiving spirits, we can also deceive ourselves. Now that you are alive in Christ, completely forgiven and totally accepted, you don't need to defend yourself the way you used to. Christ is now your defense. Confess the ways the Lord shows you that you have deceived yourself or wrongly defended yourself by using the following lists and prayers of confession:

WAYS YOU DECEIVE YOURSELF

- ☑ Hearing God's Word but not doing what it says (see James 1:22)
- ☑ Saying that I have no sin (see 1 John 1:8)
- ☑ Thinking I am something I'm really not (see Galatians 6:3)
- ☑ Thinking I am wise in this worldly age (see 1 Corinthians 3:18,19)
- ☐ Thinking I can be truly religious but not bridle my tongue (see James 1:26)

> Lord, I confess that I have deceived myself by
> _____. Thank You for Your forgiveness.
> I commit myself to believing only Your truth. In Jesus' name,
> amen.

WAYS YOU WRONGLY DEFEND YOURSELF

- ☑ Denial of reality (conscious or unconscious)
- ☑ Fantasy (escaping reality by daydreaming, watching TV or movies, listening to music, playing computer or video games, abusing drugs or alcohol, etc.)
- ☑ Emotional insulation (withdrawing from people or keeping people at a distance to avoid rejection)
- ☐ Regression (reverting back to less threatening times)
- ☐ Displaced anger (taking out frustrations on innocent people)
- ☑ Projection (blaming others for my problems)

☑ Rationalization (making excuses for my own poor behavior)
☑ Lying (presenting a false image)

Lord, I confess that I have defended myself wrongly by
_____. Thank You for Your forgiveness. I now commit myself to trusting in You to defend and protect me. In Jesus' name, amen.

Choosing the truth may be hard for you if you have been believing lies for many years. You may need some ongoing counseling to help weed out any defense mechanisms you have relied on to cope with life. Every Christian needs to learn that Christ is the only defense he or she needs. Realizing that you are already forgiven and accepted by God through Christ will help free you up to place all your dependence on Him.

Faith is the biblical response to the truth, and believing what God says is a choice we all can make. If you say, "I wish I could believe God, but I just can't," you are being deceived. Of course you can believe God because what God says is always true. Believing is something you choose to do, not something you feel like doing.

THE TRUTH ABOUT YOUR FATHER GOD

A major deception of the enemy is to cause us to equate our feelings about our Father God with the way our parents or other authority figures in our lives may have failed or mistreated us. If you harbor negative feelings from your past or present authority relationships, if you find it difficult to love or feel loved by God, if you have difficulty trusting God, it would be important for you to gain freedom from those misconceptions. A true understanding of God is foundational to your freedom. (See appendix C, p. 47.)

ARE YOU FEARFUL AND ANXIOUS?

Anxiety and plaguing fears can control our lives and prevent us from walking by faith in the surpassing victory that is ours in Christ. If you feel that anxiety and fear are preventing you from living with boldness and confidence in God's presence and power in your life, you need to renounce them specifically to gain the freedom that is yours in Christ. (See appendices D and E, pp. 49-58.)

The New Age movement has twisted the concept of faith by saying that we make something true by believing it. No, we can't create reality with our minds; only God creates reality. We can only *face* reality with our minds. Faith is choosing to believe and act upon what God says, regardless of feelings or circumstances. Believing something does not make it true. *It's true; therefore, we choose to believe it.*

Just having faith is not enough. The key question is whether the object of your faith is trustworthy. If the object of your faith is not reliable, then no amount of believing will change it. That is why our faith must be on the solid rock of God and His Word. That is the only way to live a responsible and fruitful life. On the other hand, if what you believe in is not true, then you will not experience the freedom that only the truth can bring.

For two thousand years, Christians have known the importance of publicly declaring what they believe. Read aloud the following Statement of Truth, thinking about what you are saying. You may find it very helpful to read it daily for several weeks to renew your mind with the truth and replace any lies you may be believing.

STATEMENTS OF TRUTH

1. **I recognize that there is only one true and living God who exists as the Father, Son and Holy Spirit. He is worthy of all honor, praise and glory as the One who made all things and holds all things together (see Exodus 20:2,3; Colossians 1:16,17).**

2. **I recognize that Jesus Christ is the Messiah, the Word who became flesh and dwelt among us. I believe that He came to destroy the works of the devil, and that He disarmed the rulers and authorities and made a public display of them, having triumphed over them (see John 1:1,14; Colossians 2:15; 1 John 3:8).**

3. I believe that God demonstrated His own love for me in that while I was still a sinner, Christ died for me. I believe that He has delivered me from the domain of darkness and transferred me to His kingdom, and in Him I have redemption and the forgiveness of sins (see Romans 5:8; Colossians 1:13,14).

4. I believe that I am now a child of God and that I am seated with Christ in the heavenlies. I believe that I was saved by the grace of God through faith, and that it was a gift and not a result of any works on my part (see Ephesians 2:6,8,9; 1 John 3:1-3).

5. I choose to be strong in the Lord and in the strength of His might. I put no confidence in the flesh, for the weapons of warfare are not of the flesh but are divinely powerful for the destruction of strongholds. I put on the full armor of God. I resolve to stand firm in my faith and resist the evil one (see 2 Corinthians 10:4; Ephesians 6:10-20;Phi-lippians 3:3).

6. I believe that apart from Christ I can do nothing, so I declare my complete dependence on Him. I choose to abide in Christ in order to bear much fruit and glorify my Father. I announce to Satan that Jesus is my Lord. I reject any and all counterfeit gifts or works of Satan in my life (see John 15:5,8; 1 Corinthians 12:3).

7. I believe that the truth will set me free and that Jesus is the truth. If He sets me free, I will be free indeed. I recognize that walking in the light is the only path of true fellowship with God and man. Therefore, I stand against all of Satan's deception by taking every thought captive in obedience to Christ. I declare that the Bible is the only authoritative standard for truth and life (see John 8:32,36; 14:6; 2 Corinthians 10:5; 2 Timothy 3:15-17; 1 John 1:3-7).

8. I choose to present my body to God as a living and holy sacrifice, and the members of my body as instruments of righteousness. I choose to renew my mind by the living Word of God in order that I may prove that the will of God is good, acceptable and perfect. I put off the old self with its evil practices and put on the new self.

I declare myself to be a new creation in Christ (see Romans 6:13; 12:1,2; 2 Corinthians 5:17; Colossians 3:9,10, *NIV*).

9. By faith, I choose to be filled with the Spirit so that I can be guided into all truth. I choose to walk by the Spirit so that I will not carry out the desires of the flesh (see John 16:13; Galatians 5:16; Ephesians 5:18).

10. I renounce all selfish goals and choose the ultimate goal of love. I choose to obey the two greatest commandments: to love the Lord my God with all my heart, soul, mind and strength, and to love my neighbor as myself (see Deuteronomy 6:5; Matthew 22:37-39; 1 Timothy 1:5).

11. I believe that the Lord Jesus has all authority in heaven and on earth, and He is the head over all rule and authority. I am complete in Him. I believe that Satan and his demons are subject to me in Christ since I am a member of Christ's body. Therefore, I obey the command to submit to God and resist the devil, and I command Satan in the name of Jesus Christ to leave my presence (see Matthew 28:18; Ephesians 1:19-23; Colossians 2:10; James 4:7).

STEP 3

BITTERNESS VS. FORGIVENESS

We need to forgive others so Satan cannot take advantage of us (see 2 Corinthians 2:10,11). We are commanded to get rid of all bitterness in our lives and forgive others as we have been forgiven (see Ephesians 4:31,32). Ask God to bring to your mind the people you need to forgive by praying the fol lowing prayer aloud:

> Dear Heavenly Father,
> I thank You for the riches of Your kindness, forbearance and patience toward me, knowing that Your kindness has led me to repentance.[2] I confess that I have not shown that same kindness and patience toward those who have hurt or offended me. Instead, I have held on to my anger, bitterness and resentment toward them. Please bring to my mind all the people I need to forgive in order that I may now do so. In Jesus' name, amen.

On a separate sheet of paper, list the names of people who come to your mind. At this point don't question whether you need to forgive them or not. If a name comes to mind, write it down.

Often we hold things against ourselves as well, punishing ourselves for wrong choices we've made in the past. Write "Myself" at the bottom of your list if you need to forgive yourself. Forgiving yourself is accepting the truth that God has already forgiven you in Christ. If God forgives you, you can forgive yourself!

Also write down "Thoughts Against God" at the bottom of your list. Obviously, God has never done anything wrong so we don't have to forgive Him. Sometimes, however, we harbor angry thoughts against Him because He did not do what we wanted Him to do. Those feelings of anger or resentment against God can become a wall between us and Him, so we must let them go.

Before you begin working through the process of forgiving those on your list, take a few minutes to review what forgiveness is and what it is not.

FORGIVENESS IS NOT MERELY FORGETTING

People who want to forget all that was done to them will find they cannot do it. Don't put off forgiving those who have hurt you, hoping the pain will one day go away. Once you choose to forgive someone, *then* Christ can come and begin to heal you of your hurts. But the healing cannot begin until you first forgive.

FORGIVENESS IS A CHOICE, A DECISION OF YOUR WILL

Since God requires you to forgive, it is something you can do. Sometimes it is very hard to forgive someone because we naturally want revenge for the things we have suffered. Forgiveness seems to go against our sense of what is right and fair. So we hold on to our anger, punishing people over and over again in our minds for the pain they've caused us.

But we are told by God never to take our own revenge (see Romans 12:19). Let God deal with the person. Let him or her off your hook, because as long as you refuse to forgive someone, you are still hooked to that person. You are still chained to your past, bound up in your bitterness. By forgiving, you let the other person off your hook; but he or she is not off God's hook. You must trust that God will deal with the person justly and fairly, something you simply cannot do.

"But you don't know how much this person hurt me!" you say. You're right. We don't, but Jesus does, and He tells you to forgive others for your sake. Until you let go of your anger and hatred, the person is still hurting you. You can't turn back the clock and change the past, but you can be free from it. You can stop the pain; but there is only one way to do it—forgive from your heart.

Forgive others for your sake, so you can be free from your past.

FORGIVENESS IS AGREEING TO LIVE WITH THE CONSEQUENCES OF ANOTHER'S SIN

You are going to live with those consequences whether you like it or not, so the only choice you have is whether you will do so in the bondage of bitterness or in the freedom of forgiveness. No one truly forgives without accepting and suffering the pain of another person's sin. That can seem unfair, and you may wonder, "Where is the justice?" The Cross makes forgiveness legally and morally right. Jesus died once for all our sins.

Jesus took the *eternal* consequences of sin upon Himself. God "made Him who knew no sin to be sin on our behalf, that we might become the righteousness of God in Him" (2 Corinthians 5:21). We, however, often suffer the temporary consequences of other people's sins. That is simply a harsh reality of life all of us have to face.

Do not wait for the other person to ask for your forgiveness. Remember, Jesus did not wait for those who were crucifying Him to apologize before He forgave them. Even while they mocked and jeered at Him, He prayed, "Father, forgive them, for they do not know what they are doing" (Luke 23:34, *NIV*).

FORGIVENESS COMES FROM YOUR HEART

Allow God to bring the painful memories to the surface, and then acknowledge how you feel toward those who've hurt you. If your forgiveness doesn't touch the emotional core of your life, it will be incomplete. Too often we're afraid of the pain, so we bury our emotions deep down inside us. Let God bring them to the surface so He can begin to heal those damaged emotions.

FORGIVENESS IS CHOOSING NOT TO HOLD SOMEONE'S SIN AGAINST HIM OR HER ANYMORE

It is common for bitter people to bring up past issues with those who have hurt them. They want the other people to feel as bad as they do! But we must let go of the past and choose to reject any thought of revenge. This doesn't mean you continue to put up with the future sins of others. God does not tolerate sin and neither should you. Don't allow yourself to be continually abused by others. Take a stand against sin while continuing to exercise grace and forgiveness toward those who hurt you. If you need help setting scriptural boundaries to protect yourself from further abuse, talk to a trusted friend, counselor or pastor.

FORGIVENESS CANNOT WAIT UNTIL YOU FEEL LIKE FORGIVING

You will never get there. Make the hard choice to forgive even if you don't feel like it. Once you choose to forgive, Satan will lose his power over you in that area, and God will heal your damaged emotions. Freedom is what you will gain right now, not necessarily an immediate change in feelings.

Now you are ready to begin. Starting with the first person on your list, make the choice to forgive him or her for every painful memory that comes to your mind. Continue until you are sure you have dealt with all the remembered pain caused by that individual. Then work your way down the list in the same way.

As you begin forgiving people, God may bring to your mind painful memories you've totally forgotten. Let Him do this even if it hurts. God wants you to be free; forgiving those people is the only way. Don't try to excuse the offender's behavior, even if it is someone you are really close to.

Don't say, "Lord, please help me to forgive." He is already helping you and will be with you all the way through the process. Don't say, "Lord, I want to forgive . . . " because that bypasses the hard choice we have to make. Say, "Lord, I *choose* to forgive . . . "

For every painful memory you have for each person on your list, pray aloud:

> **Lord,**
> I choose to forgive _____ (name the person) for _____ (what he/she did or failed to do), **which made me feel** _____(share the painful feelings).

After you have forgiven each person for all the offenses that came to your mind, and after you have honestly expressed how you felt, conclude this step by praying aloud:

> **Lord,**
> **I choose not to hold on to my resentment. I thank You for setting me free from the bondage of my bitterness. I relinquish my right to seek revenge and ask You to heal my damaged emotions. I now ask You to bless those who have hurt me. In Jesus' name, amen.**

STEP 4

REBELLION VS. SUBMISSION

We live in a rebellious age. Many people only obey laws and authorities when it is convenient for them. There is a general lack of respect for those in government, and Christians are often as guilty as the rest of society in fostering a critical, rebellious spirit. Certainly, we are not expected to agree with our leaders' policies that are in violation of Scripture, but we are to "honor all people, love the brotherhood, fear God, honor the king" (1 Peter 2:17).

God established all governing authorities and requires us to be submissive (see Romans 13:1-5; 1 Peter 2:13-17). Rebelling against God and the authorities He has set up is a very serious sin because it gives Satan an opportunity to attack. God requires more, however, than just the outward appearance of submission; He wants us to sincerely submit from the heart to those in authority. It is for your spiritual protection that you live under the authority of God and those He has placed over you.

The Bible makes it clear that we have two main responsibilities toward those in authority over us: to pray for them and to submit to them (see Romans 13:1-7; 1 Timothy 2:1,2). To commit yourself to that godly lifestyle, pray the following prayer aloud from your heart:

> Dear Heavenly Father,
>
> You have said in the Bible that rebellion is the same thing as witchcraft and as bad as idolatry.[3] I know I have not always been submissive, but instead I have rebelled in my heart against You and against those You have placed in authority over me. I pray that You would show me all the ways I have been rebellious. I choose now to adopt a submissive spirit and a servant's heart. In Jesus' precious name, amen.

Being under authority is clearly an act of faith! By submitting, you are trusting God to work through His established lines of authority, even when they are harsh or unkind or tell you to do something you don't want to do. There may be times when those over you abuse their authority and break the laws that are ordained by God for the protection of innocent people. In those cases, you will need to seek help from a higher authority for your protection. The laws in your state may require that such abuse be reported to the police or other governmental agency. If there is continuing abuse (physical, mental, emotional or sexual) where you live, you may need further counseling help to deal with that situation.

If authorities abuse their position by requiring you to break God's law or compromise your commitment to Him, then you need to obey God rather than man (see Acts 4:19,20). Be careful though. Don't assume that an authority is violating God's Word just because he or she tells you to do something you don't like. We all need to adopt a humble, submissive spirit to one another in the fear of Christ (see Ephesians 5:21). In addition, however, God has set up specific lines of authority to protect us and to give order to our daily lives.

As you prayerfully look over the next list, allow the Lord to show you any specific ways in which you have been rebellious to authority. Then, using the prayer of confession that follows the list, specifically confess whatever the Lord brings to your mind.

- ❏ Civil government including traffic laws, tax laws, attitude toward government officials (see Romans 13:1-7; 1 Timothy 2:1-4; 1 Peter 2:13-17)
- ❏ Parents, stepparents or legal guardians (see Ephesians 6:1-3)
- ❏ Teachers, coaches, school officials (see Romans 13:1-4)
- ❏ Employers (past and present) (see 1 Peter 2:18-23)
- ❏ Husband (see 1 Peter 3:1-4) or Wife (see Ephesians 5:21; 1 Peter 3:7) [*Note to husbands:* Take a moment and ask the Lord if your lack of love for your wife could be fostering a rebellious spirit within her. If so, confess that now as a violation of Ephesians 5:22-33.]
- ❏ Church leaders (see Hebrews 13:7)
- ❏ God (see Daniel 9:5,9)

For each way in which the Spirit of God brings to your mind that you have been rebellious, use the following prayer to specifically confess that sin:

> **Lord, I confess that I have been rebellious toward _____ (name) by _____ (say what you did specifically). Thank You for forgiving my rebellion. I choose now to be submissive and obedient to Your Word. By the shed blood of the Lord Jesus Christ, I pray that all ground gained by evil spirits in my life due to my rebellion would be canceled. In Jesus' name, amen.**

STEP 5
PRIDE VS. HUMILITY

Pride kills. It says, "I don't need God's or anyone else's help. I can handle it by myself." Oh no, you can't! We absolutely need God, and we necessarily need each other. The apostle Paul wisely wrote, "[we] worship in the Spirit of God and glory in Christ Jesus and *put no confidence in the flesh*" (Philippians 3:3, emphasis added). That is a good definition of humility: putting no confidence in the flesh, that is, in ourselves; but, rather, being *"strong in the Lord, and in the strength of His might"* (Ephesians 6:10, emphasis added). Humility is confidence properly placed in God.

Proverbs 3:5-7 expresses a similar thought: "Trust in the LORD with all your heart, and do not lean on your own understanding. In all your ways acknowledge Him, and He will make your paths straight. Do not be wise in your own eyes; fear the LORD and turn away from evil." James 4:6-10 and 1 Peter 5:1-10 also warn us that serious spiritual problems will result when we are proud. Use the following prayer to express your commitment to living humbly before God:

> Dear Heavenly Father,
> You have said that pride goes before destruction and an arrogant spirit before stumbling. I confess that I have been thinking mainly of myself and not of others. I have not denied myself, picked up my cross daily, and followed You. As a result, I have given ground to the devil in my life. I have sinned by believing I could be happy and successful on my own. I confess that I have placed my will before Yours, and I have centered my life around myself instead of You.
> I repent of my pride and selfishness and pray that all ground gained in my members by the enemies of the Lord Jesus Christ would be canceled. I choose to rely on the Holy Spirit's power and guidance so I will do nothing from selfishness or empty conceit. With humility of mind, I will regard others as more important than myself.[4] And I choose to make You, Lord, the center of my life.
> Please show me now all the specific ways in which I have lived my life in pride. Enable me through love to serve others and in honor to prefer others. I ask all of this in the gentle and humble name of Jesus, my Lord. Amen.

Having made that commitment to God in prayer, now allow Him to show you any specific ways in which you have lived in a proud manner. The following list may help you. As the Lord brings to your mind areas of pride, use the prayer following the list to guide you in your confession.

- ❏ Having a stronger desire to do my will than God's will
- ❏ Leaning too much on my own understanding and experience rather than seeking God's guidance through prayer and His Word
- ❏ Relying on my own strengths and abilities instead of depending on the power of the Holy Spirit
- ❏ Being more concerned about controlling others than in developing self-control
- ❏ Being too busy doing *important* things to take time to do little things for others
- ❏ Having a tendency to think that I have no needs
- ❏ Finding it hard to admit when I am wrong
- ❏ Being more concerned about pleasing people than pleasing God
- ❏ Being concerned about getting the credit I feel I deserve
- ❏ Thinking I am more humble, spiritual, religious or devoted than others
- ❏ Being driven to obtain recognition by attaining degrees, titles or positions
- ❏ Often feeling that my needs are more important than another person's needs
- ❏ Considering myself better than others because of my academic, artistic or athletic abilities and accomplishments
- ❏ Other ways I have thought more highly of myself than I should

For each of the above areas that has been true in your life, pray aloud:

Lord,
   I agree I have been proud in _____ (name the area). Thank You for forgiving me for my pride. I choose to humble myself before You and others. I choose to place all my confidence in You and none in my flesh. In Jesus' name, amen.

DEALING WITH PREJUDICE AND BIGOTRY

Prejudice and bigotry are other forms of pride, and ones that are all too common. Our first reaction might be to deny that these attitudes are true of us. But any awareness of prideful attitudes toward others would be good cause to prayerfully allow God to search your heart and bring to the surface anything that needs to be dealt with. (See appendix F, p. 59.)

STEP 6

BONDAGE VS. FREEDOM

Many times we feel trapped in a vicious cycle of sin-confess-sin-confess that never seems to end. We can become very discouraged and end up just giving up and giving in to the sins of our flesh. To find freedom we must follow James 4:7: "Submit therefore to God. Resist the devil and he will flee from you." We submit to God by confession of sin and repentance (turning away from sin). We resist the devil by rejecting his lies. Instead, put on the full armor of God and walk in the truth (see Ephesians 6:10-20).

Sin that has become a habit often requires help from a trusted brother or sister in Christ. James 5:16 says, "Confess your sins to one another, and pray for one another, so that you may be healed. The effective prayer of a righteous man can accomplish much." Sometimes the assurance of 1 John 1:9 is enough: "If we confess our sins, He is faithful and righteous to forgive us our sins and to cleanse us from all unrighteousness."

Remember, confession is not saying, "I'm sorry"; it is openly admitting, "I did it." Whether you need help from other people or just the accountability of walking in the light before God, pray the following prayer aloud:

> Dear Heavenly Father,
>
> You have told me to put on the Lord Jesus Christ and make no provision for the flesh in regard to its lust. I confess that I have given in to fleshly lusts that wage war against my soul. I thank You that in Christ my sins are already forgiven, but I have broken Your holy law and given the devil a chance to wage war in my body. I come to You now to confess and renounce these sins of the flesh so that I might be cleansed and set free from the bondage of sin. Please reveal to my mind all the sins of the flesh I have committed and the ways I have grieved the Holy Spirit.[5] In Jesus' holy name, amen.

The following list contains many sins of the flesh, but a prayerful examination of Mark 7:20-23; Galatians 5:19-21; Ephesians 4:25-31 and other Scripture passages will help you to be even more thorough. Look over the list below and the Scriptures just listed and ask the Holy Spirit to bring to your mind the ones you need to confess. He may reveal others to you as well. For each one the Lord shows you, pray a prayer of confession from your heart.

There is a sample prayer following the list. (Note: Sexual sins, divorce, eating disorders, substance abuse, abortion, suicidal tendencies and perfectionism will be dealt with later in this step. Further counseling help may be necessary to find complete healing and freedom in these and other areas.)

❑ Stealing   ❑ Swearing   ❑ Drunkenness
❑ Quarreling/fighting   ❑ Apathy/laziness   ❑ Cheating
❑ Jealousy/envy   ❑ Lying   ❑ Procrastination
❑ Complaining/criticism   ❑ Hatred   ❑ Greed/materialism
❑ Lustful actions   ❑ Anger   ❑ Others _____
❑ Gossip/slander   ❑ Lustful thoughts

> Lord,
> I confess that I have committed the sin of
> _____ (name the sin). Thank You for
> Your forgiveness and cleansing. I now turn away from this sin
> and turn to You, Lord. Strengthen me by Your Holy Spirit to
> obey You. In Jesus' name, amen.

It is our responsibility not to allow sin to have control over our bodies. We must not use our bodies or another person's body as an instrument of unrighteousness (see Romans 6:12,13). Sexual immorality is not only a sin against God but is sin against your body, the temple of the Holy Spirit (see 1 Corinthians 6:18,19). To find freedom from sexual bondage, begin by praying the following prayer:

> Lord,
> I ask You to bring to my mind every sexual use of my body
> as an instrument of unrighteousness so that, in Christ, I can
> renounce these sexual sins and break their bondage. In Jesus'
> name, amen.

As the Lord brings to your mind every wrong sexual use of your body, whether it was done to you (rape, incest, sexual molestation) or willingly by you (pornography, masturbation, sexual immorality), renounce every occasion:

Lord,

I renounce _____ (name the specific use of your body) with _____ (name
any other person involved). **I ask You to break that sinful bond
with** _____ (name).

After you are finished, commit your body to the Lord by praying:

Lord,

I renounce all these uses of my body as an instrument of
unrighteousness, and I admit to any willful participation. I
choose now to present my eyes, mouth, mind, heart, hands, feet
and sexual organs to You as instruments of righteousness. I present my whole body to You as a living sacrifice, holy and acceptable. I choose to reserve the sexual use of my body for marriage
only.[6]

I reject the devil's lie that my body is not clean or that it is
dirty or in any way unacceptable to You as a result of my past
sexual experiences. Lord, thank You that You have totally
cleansed and forgiven me and that You love and accept me just
the way I am. Therefore, I choose now to accept myself and my
body as clean in Your eyes. In Jesus' name, amen.

SPECIAL PRAYERS FOR SPECIAL NEEDS

DIVORCE

Lord,

I confess to You any part that I played in my divorce (ask the
Lord to show you specifics). I thank You for Your forgiveness,
and I choose not to condemn myself. I renounce the lie that
divorce affects my identity in Christ. I am a child of God, and I
reject the lie that I am a second-class Christian because of the
divorce. I reject the lie that says I am worthless, unlovable and
that my life is empty and meaningless. I am complete in Christ
who loves me and accepts me just as I am. Lord, I commit the
healing of all hurts in my life to You as I have chosen to forgive
those who have hurt me. I also place my future in Your hands
and choose to seek human companionship in Your Church. I

surrender to Your will, should there be another spouse. I pray all this in the healing name of Jesus, my Savior, Lord and closest friend, amen.

HOMOSEXUALITY

Lord,

I renounce the lie that You have created me or anyone else to be homosexual, and I agree that in Your Word You clearly forbid homosexual behavior. I choose to accept myself as a child of God, and I thank You that You created me as a man (woman). I renounce all homosexual thoughts, urges, drives and acts, and renounce all ways that Satan has used these things to pervert my relationships. I announce that I am free in Christ to relate to the opposite sex and my own sex in the way that You intended. In Jesus' name, amen.

ABORTION

Lord,

I confess that I was not a proper guardian and keeper of the life You entrusted to me, and I admit that as sin. Thank You that because of Your forgiveness, I can forgive myself. I recognize the child is in Your caring hands for all eternity. In Jesus' name, amen.

SUICIDAL TENDENCIES

Lord,

I renounce all suicidal thoughts and any attempts I've made to take my own life or in any way injure myself. I renounce the lie that life is hopeless and that I can find peace and freedom by taking my own life. Satan is a thief and comes to steal, kill and destroy. I choose life in Christ who said He came to give me life and give it abundantly.[7] Thank You for Your forgiveness that allows me to forgive myself. I choose to believe that there is always hope in Christ. In Jesus' name, amen.

DRIVENNESS AND PERFECTIONISM

Lord,

I renounce the lie that my self-worth is dependent upon my ability to perform. I announce the truth that my identity and sense of worth is found in who I am as Your child. I renounce seeking the approval and acceptance of other people, and I choose to believe that I am already approved and accepted in Christ because of His death and resurrection for me. I choose to believe the truth that I have been saved, not by deeds done in righteousness, but according to Your mercy. I choose to believe that I am no longer under the curse of the law because Christ became a curse for me. I receive the free gift of life in Christ and choose to abide in Him. I renounce striving for perfection by living under the law. By Your grace, Heavenly Father, I choose from this day forward to walk by faith in the power of Your Holy Spirit according to what You have said is true. In Jesus' name, amen.

EATING DISORDERS OR SELF-MUTILATION

Lord,

I renounce the lie that my value as a person is dependent upon my appearance or performance. I renounce cutting or abusing myself, vomiting, using laxatives or starving myself as a means of being in control, altering my appearance or trying to cleanse myself of evil. I announce that only the blood of the Lord Jesus cleanses me from sin. I realize I have been bought with a price and my body, the temple of the Holy Spirit, belongs to God. Therefore, I choose to glorify God in my body. I renounce the lie that I am evil or that any part of my body is evil. Thank You that You accept me just the way I am in Christ. In Jesus' name, amen.

SUBSTANCE ABUSE

Lord,

I confess that I have misused substances (alcohol, tobacco, food, prescription or street drugs) for the purpose of pleasure, to escape reality or to cope with difficult problems. I confess that I have abused my body and programmed my mind in a harmful way. I have quenched the Holy Spirit as well. Thank You for forgiving me. I renounce any satanic connection or influence in my life through my misuse of food or chemicals. I cast my anxieties onto Christ who loves me. I commit myself to yield no longer to substance abuse, but instead I choose to allow the Holy Spirit to direct and empower me. In Jesus' name, amen.

STEP 7

CURSES VS. BLESSINGS

The next step to freedom is to renounce the sins of your ancestors as well as any satanic assignments directed toward you or your ministry. In the Ten Commandments, God said:

> You shall not make for yourself an idol, or any likeness of what is in heaven above or on the earth beneath or in the water under the earth. You shall not worship them or serve them; for I, the LORD your God, am a jealous God, visiting the iniquity of the fathers on the children, on the third and the fourth generations of those who hate Me, but showing loving kindness to thousands, to those who love Me and keep My commandments (Exodus 20:4-6).

The iniquities of one generation can adversely affect future generations unless the sins of the ancestors are confessed and renounced, and your spiritual heritage in Christ is claimed. You are not guilty for the sin of your ancestors, but because of their sin, you may be predisposed to certain strengths or weaknesses and influenced by the physical and spiritual atmosphere in which you were raised. These conditions can contribute to causing someone to struggle with a particular sin. Ask the Lord to show you specifically what sins are characteristic of your family by praying the following prayer:

Dear Heavenly Father,
    I ask You to reveal to my mind now all the sins of my ancestors that are being passed down through family lines. I want to be free from those influences and walk in my new identity as a child of God. In Jesus' name, amen.

As the Lord brings those areas of family sin to your mind, list them below. You will be specifically renouncing them later in this step.

In order to walk free from the sins of your ancestors and any assignments targeted against you, read the following declaration and pray the following prayer aloud. Remember, you have all the authority and protection you need in Christ to take your stand against such activity.

DECLARATION

I here and now reject and disown all the sins of my ancestors. I specifically renounce the sins of _____ (name the areas of family sin the Lord revealed to you). As one who has now been delivered from the domain of darkness into the kingdom of God's Son, I choose to believe that all the sins and iniquities of my ancestors have been confessed and I now stand forgiven and cleansed in Christ. As one who has been crucified and raised with Jesus Christ and who sits with Him in heavenly places, I renounce all satanic assignments that are directed toward me and my ministry. I choose to believe that Jesus has broken every curse that Satan and his workers have put on me. I announce to Satan and all his forces that Christ became a curse for me when He died for my sins on the Cross.[8] I reject any and every way in which Satan may claim ownership of me. I belong to the Lord Jesus Christ who purchased me with His own blood. I reject all blood sacrifices whereby Satan may claim ownership of me. I declare myself to be fully and eternally signed over and committed to the Lord Jesus Christ. By the authority I have in Christ, I now command every enemy of the Lord Jesus to leave my presence. I commit myself to my Heavenly Father to do His will from this day forward. In Jesus' name, amen.

PRAYER

Dear Heavenly Father,

I come to You as Your child, bought out of slavery to sin by the blood of the Lord Jesus Christ. You are the Lord of the universe and the Lord of my life. I submit my body to You as an instrument of righteousness, a living and holy sacrifice that I may glorify You in my body. I now ask You to fill me to overflowing with Your Holy Spirit today and everyday. I commit myself to the renewing of my mind in order to prove that Your will is good, acceptable and perfect for me. All this I pray in the name and authority of the risen Lord Jesus Christ. Amen.

Maintaining Your Freedom

Even after finding freedom in Christ by going through these seven steps, you may come under attack hours, days or even weeks later. But you don't have to yield to the world, the flesh or the devil. As you continue to walk in humble submission to God, you can resist the devil and he will flee from you (see James 4:7).

The devil is attracted to sin like flies are attracted to garbage. Get rid of the garbage, and the flies will depart for smellier places. In the same way, walk in the truth, confessing all sin and forgiving those who hurt you, and the devil will have no place in your life.

Realize that one victory does not mean the battles are over. Freedom must be maintained. After completing these steps to freedom, one happy lady asked, "Will I always be like this?" The answer is, she will maintain her freedom as long as she remains in a right relationship with God. Even if she slips and falls, she should know how to get right with God again.

One victim of horrible atrocities shared this illustration:

> It was like being forced to play a game with an ugly stranger in my own home. I kept losing and wanting to quit, but the ugly stranger wouldn't let me. Finally, I called the police (a higher authority), and they came and escorted the stranger out. He knocked on the door, trying to regain entry, but this time I recognized his voice and didn't let him in.

What a beautiful picture of gaining and keeping your freedom in Christ! We call upon Jesus, the ultimate authority, and He escorts the enemy of our souls away from us.

How to Maintain Your Freedom

Your freedom must be maintained. We cannot emphasize that enough. You have won a very important battle in an ongoing war. Freedom will continue to be yours as long as you keep choosing the truth and standing firm in the strength of the Lord. If you become aware of lies you have believed, renounce them and choose the truth. If new, painful memories surface, forgive those who hurt you. If the Lord shows you other areas of sin in your life, confess those promptly. This book can serve as a constant guide for you in dealing with the things God points out to you. Some people have found it helpful to walk through the Steps to Freedom in Christ again. As you do, read the instructions carefully.

For your encouragement and growth, we recommend that you read *Victory over the Darkness* (or the youth version, *Stomping Out the Darkness*), *Walking in Freedom* (a 21-day follow-up devotional) and *Who I Am in Christ*. To maintain your freedom in Christ, we strongly suggest the following as well:

1. Be involved in a loving, caring church fellowship where you can be open and honest with others and where God's truth is taught with grace.

2. Read and meditate on the Bible daily. Memorize key verses from these Steps to Freedom in Christ. You may want to read the Statement of Truth (see Step 2, p.12) aloud daily and study the verses mentioned.

3. Learn to take every thought captive to the obedience of Christ. Assume responsibility for your thought life. Don't let your mind become passive. Reject all lies, choose to focus on the truth and stand firm in your true identity as a child of God in Christ.

4. Don't drift back to old patterns of thinking, feeling and acting. This can happen very easily if you become spiritually and mentally lazy. If you are struggling with walking in the truth, share your battles openly with a trusted friend who will pray for you and encourage you to stand firm.

5. Don't expect other people to fight your battles for you, however. They can help you, but they can't think, pray, read the Bible or choose the truth for you.

6. Commit yourself to daily prayer. Prayer demonstrates a life of trusting in and depending on God. You can pray the following prayers often and with confidence. Let the words come from your heart as well as your lips, and feel free to change them to make them *your* prayers.

DAILY PRAYER AND DECLARATION

Dear Heavenly Father,

I praise You and honor You as my Lord and Savior. You are in control of all things. I thank You that You are always with me and will never leave me nor forsake me. You are the only all-powerful and only wise God. You are kind and loving in all Your ways. I love You and thank You that I am united with Christ and spiritually alive in Him. I choose not to love the world or the things in the world, and I crucify the flesh and all its passions.

Thank You for the life I now have in Christ. I ask You to fill me with the Holy Spirit so I may say no to sin and yes to You. I declare my total dependence upon You, and I take my stand against Satan and all his lying ways. I choose to believe the truth of God's Word despite what my feelings may say. I refuse to be discouraged; You are the God of all hope. Nothing is too difficult for You. I am confident that You will supply all my needs as I seek to live according to Your Word. I thank You that I can be content and live a responsible life through Christ who strengthens me.

I now take my stand against Satan and command him and all his evil spirits to depart from me. I choose to put on the full armor of God so that I might be able to stand firm against the devil's schemes. I submit my body as a living and holy sacrifice to God, and I choose to renew my mind by the living Word of God. By so doing I will be able to prove that the will of God is good, acceptable and perfect for me. In the name of my Lord and Savior, Jesus Christ, amen.

BEDTIME PRAYER

Thank You, Lord, that You have brought me into Your family and have blessed me with every spiritual blessing in the heavenly places in Christ Jesus. Thank You for this time of renewal and refreshment through sleep. I accept it as one of Your blessings for Your children, and I trust You to guard my mind and my body during my sleep.

As I have thought about You and Your truth during the day, I choose to let those good thoughts continue in my mind while I am asleep. I commit myself to You for Your protection against every attempt of Satan and his demons to attack me during sleep. Guard my mind from nightmares. I renounce all fear and cast every anxiety upon You, Lord. I commit myself to You as my rock, my fortress and my strong tower. May Your peace be upon this place of rest now. In the strong name of the Lord Jesus Christ, amen.

PRAYER FOR CLEANSING HOME/APARTMENT/ROOM

After removing and destroying all objects of false worship, pray this prayer aloud in every room if necessary:

Heavenly Father,

I acknowledge that You are the Lord of heaven and earth. In Your sovereign power and love, You have given me all things to enjoy. Thank You for this place to live. I claim my home as a place of spiritual safety for me and my family and ask for Your protection from all the attacks of the enemy. As a child of God, raised up and seated with Christ in the heavenly places, I command every evil spirit claiming ground in this place, based on the activities of past or present occupants, including me, to leave and never return. I renounce all curses and spells directed against this place. I ask You, Heavenly Father, to post Your holy, warring angels around this place to guard it from any and all attempts of the enemy to enter and disturb Your purposes for me and my family. I thank You, Lord, for doing this in the name of the Lord Jesus Christ, amen.

PRAYER FOR LIVING IN A NON-CHRISTIAN ENVIRONMENT

After removing and destroying all objects of false worship from your possession, pray this aloud in the place where you live:

Thank You, Heavenly Father, for a place to live and to be renewed by sleep. I ask You to set aside my room (or portion of this room) as a place of spiritual safety for me. I renounce any allegiance given to false gods or spirits by other occupants. I renounce any claim to this room (space) by Satan based on the activities of past or present occupants, including me. On the basis of my position as a child of God and joint heir with Christ, who has all authority in heaven and on earth, I command all evil spirits to leave this place and never return. I ask You, Heavenly Father, to station Your holy, warring angels to protect me while I live here. In Jesus' mighty name, amen.

Continue to walk in the truth that your identity and sense of worth comes through who you are in Christ. Renew your mind with the truth that your acceptance, security and significance are in Christ alone.

We recommend that you meditate on the following truths daily. Try reading the entire list aloud, morning and evening, for the next few weeks. Think about what you are reading and let your heart rejoice in the truth.

IN CHRIST

I renounce the lie that I am rejected, unloved, dirty or shameful because in Christ I am completely accepted. God says that

I am God's child (see John 1:12).

I am Christ's friend (see John 15:15).

I have been justified (see Romans 5:1).

I am united with the Lord and I am one spirit with Him (see 1 Corinthians 6:17).

I have been bought with a price; I belong to God (see 1 Corinthians 6:19,20).

I am a member of Christ's body (see 1 Corinthians 12:27).

I am a saint, a holy one (see Ephesians 1:1).

I have been adopted as God's child (see Ephesians 1:5).

I have direct access to God through the Holy Spirit (see Ephesians 2:18).

I have been redeemed and forgiven of all my sins (see Colossians 1:14).

I am complete in Christ (see Colossians 2:10).

I renounce the lie that I am guilty, unprotected, alone or abandoned because in Christ I am totally secure. God says that

I am free forever from condemnation (see Romans 8:1,2).

I am assured that all things work together for good (see Romans 8:28).

I am free from any condemning charges against me (see Romans 8:31-34).

I cannot be separated from the love of God (see Romans 8:35-39).

I have been established, anointed and sealed by God (see 2 Corinthians 1:21,22).

I am confident that the good work God has begun in me will be perfected (see Philippians 1:6).

I am a citizen of heaven (see Philippians 3:20).

I am hidden with Christ in God (see Colossians 3:3).

I have not been given a spirit of fear, but of power, love and a sound mind (see 2 Timothy 1:7).

I can find grace and mercy to help in time of need (see Hebrews 4:16).

I am born of God, and the evil one cannot touch me (see 1 John 5:18).

I renounce the lie that I am worthless, inadequate, helpless or hopeless because in Christ I am deeply significant. God says that

I am the salt of the earth and the light of the world (see Matthew 5:13,14).

I am a branch of the true vine, Jesus, a channel of His life (see John 15:1,5).

I have been chosen and appointed by God to bear fruit (see John 15:16).

I am a personal, Spirit-empowered witness of Christ's (see Acts 1:8).

I am a temple of God (see 1 Corinthians 3:16).

I am a minister of reconciliation for God (see 2 Corinthians 5:17-21).

I am God's coworker (see 2 Corinthians 6:1).

I am seated with Christ in the heavenly realm (see Ephesians 2:6).

I am God's workmanship, created for good works (see Ephesians 2:10).

I may approach God with freedom and confidence (see Ephesians 3:12).

I can do all things through Christ who strengthens me! (see Philippians 4:13).

I am not the great "I AM," but by the grace of God I am what I am. (See Exodus 3:14; John 8:24,28,58; 1 Corinthians 15:10.)

SEEKING THE FORGIVENESS OF OTHERS

Now that you have found your freedom in Christ, there may be an additional step for you to take. In Step 3 you dealt with the need to forgive others who have offended you. You may need to seek the forgiveness of those you have offended. You need to know if and when to take that further step and how to do it in a wise and godly manner. (See appendix G, p. 61.)

APPENDIX A

EVALUATE YOUR PRIORITIES

Who or what is most important to us becomes that which we worship. Our thoughts, love, devotion, trust, adoration and obedience are directed to this object of person above all others. Our worship may end up being directed toward the true God or diverted toward other gods.

We were created to worship the true and living God. In fact, the Father seeks those who will worship Him in spirit and in truth (see John 4:23). As children of God, "we know also that the Son of God has come and has given us understanding, so that we may know him who is true. And we are in him who is true—even in his Son Jesus Christ. He is the true God and eternal life" (1 John 5:20, NIV).

The apostle John follows the above passage with a warning: "Little children, guard yourselves from idols" (1 John 5:21). An idol is a false god, any object of worship other than the true God. Though we may not bow down to statues, it is easy for people and things of this world to subtly become more important to us than our relationship with God. The following prayer expresses the commitment of a heart that chooses to "worship the LORD your GOD, and serve Him only" (Matthew 4:10):

> Dear Lord God,
> I know how easy it is to allow other things and other people to become more important to me than You. I also know that this is offensive to Your holy eyes as You have commanded that I should have no other gods before You.
> I confess to You that I have not loved You with all my heart and soul and mind. As a result, I have sinned against You, violating the first and greatest commandment. I repent of and turn away from this idolatry and now choose to return to You, Lord Jesus, as my first love.[9]
> Please reveal to my mind any and all idols in my life. I choose to renounce every idol that would give Satan any right in my life. In the name of Jesus, the true God, amen.

The following checklist may help you recognize those areas where things or people have become more important to you than the true God, Jesus Christ. Notice that most (if not all) of the areas listed below are not evil in themselves; they become idols when they usurp God's rightful place as Lord of our lives.

- ❏ Ambition
- ❏ Food or any substance
- ❏ Money/possessions
- ❏ Computers/games/software
- ❏ Financial security
- ❏ Rock stars/media celebrities/athletes
- ❏ Church activities
- ❏ TV/movies/music/other media
- ❏ Sports or physical fitness
- ❏ Fun/pleasure
- ❏ Ministry
- ❏ Appearance/image

- ❏ Work
- ❏ Busyness/activity
- ❏ Friends
- ❏ Power/control
- ❏ Boyfriend/girlfriend
- ❏ Popularity/opinion of others
- ❏ Spouse
- ❏ Knowledge/being right
- ❏ Children
- ❏ Hobbies
- ❏ Parents
- ❏ Others _____

Use the following prayer to renounce any areas of idolatry or wrong priority the Holy Spirit brings to your mind:

> **In the name of the Lord Jesus Christ, I confess that I have made** _____ (person or thing) **more important than You, and I renounce that false worship. I choose to worship only You, Lord. I ask You, Father, to enable me to keep this area of** _____ (name the idol) **in its proper place in my life. In Jesus' name, amen.**

APPENDIX B

SATANIC RITUALS OR HEAVY OCCULT ACTIVITY

If you have been involved in satanic rituals or heavy occult activity or you suspect it because of blocked memories, severe and recurring nightmares, or sexual bondage or dysfunction, we strongly urge you to say aloud the Special Renunciations for Satanic Ritual Involvement. Read across the page, renouncing the first item in the column under Domain of Darkness and then announcing the first truth in the column under Kingdom of Light. Continue down the page in that manner.

In addition to the Special Renunciations list, all other satanic rituals, covenants (promises) and assignments must be specifically renounced as the Lord brings them to your mind.

Some people who have been subjected to Satanic Ritual Abuse (SRA) develop multiple or alternate personalities in order to cope with their pain. If this is true in your case, you need someone who understands spiritual conflict to help you work through this problem. For now, walk through the rest of the Steps to Freedom in Christ as best you can. It is important that you remove any demonic strongholds in your life *before* trying to integrate the personalities. Every personality that surfaces must be acknowledged and guided into resolving his or her issues; then all true personalities can agree to come together in Christ.

SPECIAL RENUNCIATIONS FOR SATANIC RITUAL INVOLVEMENT

Kingdom of Darkness	Kingdom of Light
I renounce ever signing my name over to Satan or having had my name signed over to Satan.	I announce that my name is now written in the Lamb's Book of Life.
I renounce any ceremony where I may have been wed to Satan.	I announce that I am the bride of Christ.
I renounce any and all covenants that I made with Satan.	I announce that I am a partaker of the New Covenant with Christ.
I renounce all satanic assignments for my life, including duties, marriage and children.	I announce and commit myself to know and do only the will of God and accept only His guidance.
I renounce all spirit guides assigned to me.	I announce and accept only the leading of the Holy Spirit.
I renounce ever giving my blood in the service of Satan.	I trust only in the shed blood of my Lord Jesus Christ.
I renounce ever eating flesh or drinking blood for satanic worship	By faith I eat only the flesh and drink only the blood of Jesus in Holy Communion.
I renounce any and all guardians and satanist parents who were assigned to me.	I announce that God is my Father and the Holy Spirit is my Guardian by which I am sealed.
I renounce any baptism in blood or urine whereby I am identified with Satan.	I announce that I have been baptized into Christ Jesus and my identity is now in Christ.
I renounce any and all sacrifices that were made on my behalf by which Satan may claim ownership of me.	I announce that only the sacrifice of Christ has any hold on me. I belong to Him. I have been purchased by the blood of the Lamb.

APPENDIX C

THE TRUTH ABOUT YOUR FATHER GOD

Sometimes we are greatly hindered from walking by faith in our Father God because of lies we have believed about Him. We are to have a healthy fear of God—awe of His holiness, power and presence—but we no longer need to fear punishment from Him. Romans 8:15 says, "For you have not received a spirit of slavery leading to fear again, but you have received a spirit of adoption as sons by which we cry out, 'Abba! Father!' " The following exercise will help break the chains of those lies and enable you to begin to experience that intimate "Abba, Father" relationship with Him.

Work your way down the lists on the following page one by one, left to right. Begin each one with the statement in bold at the top of that list. Read through the lists *aloud*.

I renounce the lie that my Father God is . . .	I joyfully accept the truth that my Father God is . . .
distant and disinterested	intimate and involved (see Psalm 139:1-18)
insensitive and uncaring	kind and compassionate (see Psalm 103:8-14)
stern and demanding	accepting and filled with joy and love (see Romans 15:7; Zephaniah 3:17)
passive and cold	warm and affectionate (see Isaiah 40:11; Hosea 11:3,4)
absent or too busy for me	always with me and eager to be with me (see Hebrews 13:5; Jeremiah 31:20; Ezekiel 34:11-16)
never satisfied with what I do, impatient or angry	patient and slow to anger (see Exodus 34:6; 2 Peter 3:9)
mean, cruel or abusive	loving, gentle and protective of me (see Jeremiah 31:3; Isaiah 42:3; Psalm 18:2)
trying to take all the fun out of life	trustworthy and wants to give me a full life; His will is good, perfect and acceptable for me (see Lamentations 3:22,23; John 10:10; Romans 12:1,2)
controlling or manipulative	full of grace and mercy, and He gives me freedom to fail (see Hebrews 4:15,16; Luke 15:11-16)
condemning or unforgiving	tender-hearted and forgiving; His heart and arms are always open to me (see Psalm 130:1-4; Luke 15:17-24)
nit-picking, exacting or perfectionistic	committed to my growth and proud of me as His growing child (see Romans 8:28,29; Hebrews 12:5-11; 2 Corinthians 7:14)
I am the apple of His eye! (See Deuteronomy 32:9,10.)	

APPENDIX D

RESOLVING ANXIETY

Anxiety is different from fear in that it lacks an object or adequate cause. People are anxious because they are uncertain about a specific outcome or don't know what is going to happen tomorrow. It is normal to be concerned about things we value; to not do so would demonstrate a lack of care.

One can be temporarily anxious about an examination yet to be taken, attendance at a planned function or the threat of an incoming storm. Such concern is normal and should ordinarily move one to responsible action. For some, the anxiety is more intense and prolonged. They struggle with a large number of worries and spend a lot of time and energy doing so. The intensity and frequency of the worrying are always out of proportion to the actual problem.

If persistent anxiety is a problem in your life, this Anxiety Worksheet can help you to cast all your anxieties on Christ because he cares for you (see 1 Peter 5:7).

PRAY

Prayer is the first step in casting all your anxiety on Christ. Remember Paul's words, "Be anxious for nothing, but in everything by prayer and supplication with thanksgiving let your requests be made known to God" (Philippians 4:6). Ask God to guide you by expressing the following prayer:

> Dear Heavenly Father,
> I come to You as your child, purchased by the blood of the Lord Jesus Christ. I declare my dependence upon You, and I acknowledge my need of You. I know that apart from Christ I can do nothing. You know the thoughts and intentions of my heart, and You know the situation I am in from the beginning to the end. I feel as though I am double-minded, and I need your peace to guard my heart and my mind. I humble myself before You and choose to trust You to exalt me at the proper time in any way You choose. I place my trust in You to supply all my needs according to Your riches in glory and to guide me into all truth. I ask for Your divine guidance so that I may fulfill my calling to live a responsible life by faith in the power of Your Holy Spirit. "Search me, O God, and know my heart; try

me and know my anxious thoughts; and see if there be any hurtful way in me, and lead me in the everlasting way."[10] In Jesus' precious name, amen.

RESOLVE ANY PERSONAL AND SPIRITUAL CONFLICTS

The purpose of the Steps to Freedom in Christ is to help you get radically right with God and eliminate any possible influences of the devil on your mind. Remember, "The Spirit clearly says that in later times some will abandon the faith and follow deceiving spirits and things taught by demons" (1 Timothy 4:1, NIV). You will be a double-minded person if you pay attention to a deceiving spirit. You need to have the presence of God in order to have "the peace of God, which surpasses all comprehension, will guard your hearts and your minds in Christ Jesus" (Philippians 4:7).

STATE THE PROBLEM

A problem well-stated is half-solved. In anxious states of mind, people typically can't see the forest for the trees. Put the problem in perspective: Will it matter for eternity? Generally speaking, the process of worrying takes a greater toll on a person than the negative consequences of what they worried about. Many anxious people find tremendous relief by simply having their problem clarified and put into perspective.

DIVIDE THE FACTS FROM THE ASSUMPTIONS

People may be fearful of the facts but not anxious. Fear has an object, and we'll be dealing with that in the following exercise. We're anxious because we don't know what is going to happen tomorrow. Since we don't know, we make assumptions. A peculiar trait of the mind is its tendency to assume the worst. If the assumption is accepted as truth, it will drive the mind to its anxiety limits. If you make presumptions about tomorrow, you will suffer the negative consequences, or stress and anxiety. "Anxiety in the heart of a man weighs it down" (Proverbs 12:25). Therefore, as best as possible, verify all assumptions.

DETERMINE WHAT YOU HAVE THE RIGHT OR ABILITY TO CONTROL

You are responsible only for that which you have the right and ability to control. You are not responsible for that which you don't. Your sense of worth is tied only to that for which you are responsible. If you aren't living a responsible life, you should feel anxious! Don't try to cast your responsibility onto Christ—He will throw it back to you. But do cast your anxiety onto Him because His integrity is at stake in meeting your needs if you are living a responsible and righteous life.

LIST WHAT IS YOUR RESPONSIBILITY
You need to commit yourself to be a responsible person and fulfill your calling and obligations in life.

THE REST IS GOD'S RESPONSIBILITY
Your only remaining responsibility is to continue to pray and focus on the truth according to Philippians 4:6-8. Any residual anxiety is probably due to your assuming responsibilities that God never intended you to have.

ANXIETY WORKSHEET

Go to God in prayer.

Resolve all known personal and spiritual conflicts.

State the problem.

Divide the facts from assumptions.

- Facts relating to the situation:

- Assumptions relating to the situation:

Which assumptions can be verified as facts?

Determine what you have the right or ability to control.

- What you can control as a matter of personal responsibility:

- What you have no right or ability to control:

List everything related to the situation that is your responsibility.

If you have fulfilled your responsibility, the rest is God's responsibility, except for your continuing walk with Him in prayer according to Philippians 4:6-8.

APPENDIX E

STEPS TO OVERCOMING FEARS

If you have successfully resolved your personal and spiritual conflicts by submitting to God and resisting the devil, then you are ready to analyze your fears and work out a responsible course of action.

ANALYZE YOUR FEAR UNDER GOD'S AUTHORITY AND GUIDANCE

Begin by praying the following prayer aloud:

> Dear Heavenly Father,
>
> I come to You as Your child. I put myself under Your protective care and acknowledge that You are the only legitimate fear object in my life. I confess that I have been fearful and anxious because of my lack of trust and unbelief. I have not always lived by faith in You and too often I have relied on my own strength and resources. I thank You that I am forgiven in Christ.
>
> I choose to believe the truth that You have not given me a spirit of fear, but of power, love and a sound mind.[11] Therefore I renounce any spirit of fear. I ask You to reveal to my mind all the fears that have been controlling me. Show me how I have become fearful and the lies I have believed. I desire to live a responsible life in the power of Your Holy Spirit. Show me how these fears have kept me from doing that. I ask this so that I can confess, renounce and overcome every fear by faith in You. In Jesus' name, amen.

The following list may help you recognize some of the fears that have been hindering your walk of faith. On a separate sheet, write down the ones that apply to you, as well as any others not on the list that the Spirit of God has revealed to you. As you prayerfully recall your past, write a brief description of what happened, and when, to trigger that fear.

- ❏ Fear of Satan
- ❏ Fear of divorce
- ❏ Fear of death
- ❏ Fear of not being loved by God
- ❏ Fear of never being loved
- ❏ Fear of disapproval
- ❏ Fear of embarrassment
- ❏ Fear of failure
- ❏ Fear of being/becoming homo-sexual
- ❏ Fear of financial problems
- ❏ Fear of going crazy
- ❏ Fear of being a hopeless case
- ❏ Fear of the death of a loved one
- ❏ Fear of the future
- ❏ Fear of confrontation
- ❏ Fear of being victimized by crime
- ❏ Fear of having committed the unpardonable sin
- ❏ Fear of specific people, animals or objects
- ❏ Fear of not being able to love others
- ❏ Fear of marriage
- ❏ Fear of rejection by people
- ❏ Fear of never getting married
- ❏ Fear of never having children
- ❏ Other specific fears the Lord brings to mind _____

The root of any unreasonable fear is a belief that is not based in truth. These false beliefs need to be rooted out and replaced by the truth of God's Word. Take as much time in prayer as you need to discern these lies because renouncing them and choosing the truth is a critical step toward gaining and maintaining your freedom in Christ. You have to know and choose to believe the truth in order for it to set you free. Write down the lies you have believed for every fear and the corresponding truth from the Word of God.

WAYS YOU HAVE BEEN LIVING UNDER THE CONTROL OF FEAR

The next step is to determine how fear has prevented you from living a responsible life, compelled you to do that which is irresponsible or compromised your Christian witness. After you have gained the necessary insights into your fear, it is time to experience God's cleansing through confession and repentance (see 1 John 1:9; Proverbs 28:13). Confession is agreeing with God that what you did was sinful. Repentance is the choice to turn away from sin and walk by faith in God. Express the following prayer for each of the controlling fears that you have analyzed above:

Dear Lord,

I confess and repent of the fear of _____.
I have believed (state the lie). I renounce that lie, and I choose
to believe the truth (state the truth). I also confess any and all
ways this fear has resulted in living irresponsibly, or compro-
mising my witness for Christ—be specific.

I now choose to live by faith in You, Lord, believing Your
promise that You will protect me and meet all my needs as I
live by faith in You.[12] In Jesus' trustworthy name, amen.

After working through every fear the Lord has revealed to you (including the
accompanying lies and sinful behaviors), pray the following prayer:

Dear Heavenly Father,

I thank You that You are indeed trustworthy. I choose to
believe You, even when my feelings and circumstances tell me
to fear. You have told me not to fear, for You are with me,
and to not anxiously look about me, for You are my God. You
will strengthen me, help me and surely uphold me with Your
righteous right hand.[13] In Jesus' mighty name, amen.

WORK OUT A PLAN OF RESPONSIBLE BEHAVIOR

The next step is to face the fear and prayerfully work out a plan to overcome
it. Mark Twain once said, "Do the thing you fear the most and the death of fear
is certain." Fear is like a mirage in the desert. It seems so real until you move
toward it, but then it disappears into thin air. But as long as we back away from
fear, it will haunt us and grow in size, becoming like a giant.

Determine in Advance What Your Response Will Be to Any Fear Object

The fear of God is the one fear that can dispel all other fears, because God
rules supreme over every other fear object, including Satan. Even though
"your adversary, the devil, prowls about like a roaring lion, seeking someone
to devour" (1 Peter 5:8), he has been defeated. "Having disarmed the powers
and authorities, [Jesus] made a public spectacle of them, triumphing over
them by the cross" (Colossians 2:15, NIV).

The presence of any fear object should prompt us to focus on God who
is both omnipresent (always present) and omnipotent (all powerful). To
worship God is to acknowledge and ascribe to Him His divine attributes. This

keeps fresh in our minds the truth that our loving heavenly Father is always with us and is more powerful than any enemy or circumstance.

Commit to Carrying Out the Plan of Action in the Power of the Holy Spirit
Remember, you are never alone in the battle. "It is God who works in you to will and to act according to his good purpose" (Philippians 2:13, *NIV*).

FEAR FINDER

Analyze your fear under God's authority and guidance.

Identify all fear objects (i.e., what you are afraid of).

When did you first experienced each fear?

What events preceded the first experience?

What are the lies behind every fear?

Determine the ways you have been living under the control of fear rather than living by faith in God.

How has fear

- Prevented you from doing what is right and responsible?

- Compelled you to do what is wrong and irresponsible?

- Prompted you to compromise your witness for Christ?

Confess any active or passive way in which you have allowed fear to control your life.

Commit yourself to God to live a righteous and responsible life.

Prayerfully work out a plan of responsible behavior.

Determine in advance what your response will be to any fear object.

Commit yourself to carry out the plan of action in the power of the Holy Spirit.

APPENDIX F

DEALING WITH PREJUDICE AND BIGOTRY

Pride is the original sin of Lucifer. It sets one person or group against another. Satan's strategy is always to divide and conquer, but God has given us a ministry of reconciliation (see 2 Corinthians 5:19). Consider for a moment the work of Christ in breaking down the long-standing barrier of racial prejudice between Jew and Gentile.

> For [Christ] is our peace, who has made the two one and has destroyed the barrier, the dividing wall of hostility, by abolishing in his flesh the law with its commandments and regulations. His purpose was to create in himself one new man out of the two, thus making peace, and in this one body to reconcile both of them to God through the cross, by which he put to death their hostility. He came and preached peace to you who were far away and peace to those who were near. For through him we both have access to the Father by one Spirit (Ephesians 2:14-18, NIV).

Many times we deny that there is prejudice or bigotry in our hearts, yet "nothing in all creation is hidden from God's sight. Everything is uncovered and laid bare before the eyes of him to whom we must give account" (Hebrews 4:13, NIV). The following is a prayer asking God to shine His light upon your heart and reveal any area of proud prejudice:

Dear Heavenly Father,

I know that You love all people equally and that You do not show favoritism. You accept people from every nation who fear You and do what is right. You do not judge them based on skin color, race, economic standing, ethnic background, gender, denominational preference or any other worldly matter. I confess that I have too often prejudged others or regarded myself superior. I have not always been a minister of reconciliation but have been a proud agent of division through my attitudes, words and deeds. I repent of all hateful bigotry and proud prejudice, and I ask You, Lord, to now reveal to my mind all the specific ways in which this form of pride has corrupted my heart and mind.[14] In Jesus' name, amen.

For each area of prejudice, superiority or bigotry that the Lord brings to mind, pray the following prayer aloud from your heart:

Dear Heavenly Father,

I confess and renounce the prideful sin of prejudice against _____ (name the group). I thank You for Your forgiveness, Lord and ask now that You would change my heart and make me a loving agent of reconciliation with _____ (name the group). In Jesus' name, amen.

APPENDIX G

SEEKING THE FORGIVENESS OF OTHERS

Therefore, if you bring your gift to the altar, and there remember that your brother has something against you, leave your gift there before the altar, and go your way. First be reconciled to your brother, and then come and offer your gift. Agree with your adversary quickly, while you are on the way with him, lest your adversary deliver you to the judge, the judge hand you over to the officer, and you are thrown into prison. Assuredly, I say to you, you will by no means get out of there till you have paid the last penny (Matthew 5:23-26, NKJV).

THE MOTIVATION FOR SEEKING FORGIVENESS
Matthew 5:23-26 is the key passage on seeking forgiveness. Several points in this passage bear emphasizing. The worshiper coming before God to offer a gift remembers that someone has something against him. The Holy Spirit is the One who brings to his or her mind the wrong that was done.

Only the actions which have hurt another person need to be confessed to them. If you have had jealous, lustful or angry thoughts toward another, and they don't know about it, these are to be confessed to God alone.

An exception to this principle occurs when restitution needs to be made. If you stole or broke something, damaged someone's reputation, and so on, you need to go to that person and make it right, even if he or she is unaware of what you did.

THE PROCESS OF SEEKING FORGIVENESS
1. Write out what you did wrong and why you did it.
2. Make sure you have already forgiven the person for whatever he or she may have done to you.
3. Think through exactly how you will ask him or her to forgive you. Be sure to
   a. Label your action as wrong.
   b. Be specific and admit what you did.

    c.   Make no defenses or excuses.

    d.   Do not blame the other person, and do not expect or demand that he or she ask for your forgiveness.

    e.   Your confession should lead to the direct question: "Will you forgive me?"

4. Seek the right place and the right time to approach the offended person.

5. Ask for forgiveness in person from anyone with whom you can talk face-to-face with the following exception: *Do not* go alone when your safety might be in danger.

6. Except where no other means of communication is possible, *do not* write a letter because a letter can be very easily misread or misunderstood; a letter can be read by the wrong people (those having nothing to do with the offense or the confession); a letter can be kept when it should have been destroyed.

Once you sincerely seek forgiveness, you are free—whether the other person forgives you or not (see Romans 12:18).

After seeking forgiveness, fellowship with God in worship (see Matthew 5:24).

ENDNOTES

1. Psalm 139:23,24.
2. See Romans 2:4.
3. See 1 Samuel 15:23.
4. See Proverbs 16:18; Matthew 6:33; 16:24; Romans 12:10; Philippians 2:3.
5. See Proverbs 28:13, *NIV*; Romans 6:12,13; 13:14; 2 Corinthians 4:2; James 4:1; 1 Peter 2:11; 5:8.
6. See Hebrews 13:4.
7. See John 10:10.
8. See Galatians 3:13.
9. See Exodus 20:3; Matthew 22:37; Revelation 2:4,5.
10. Psalm 139:23,24.
11. See 2 Timothy 1:7.
12. See Psalm 27:1; Matthew 6:33,34.
13. See Isaiah 41:10.
14. See Acts 10:34; 2 Corinthians 5:16.

Freedom in Christ Resources

Victory over the Darkness
by Neil Anderson
Start here! This best-seller combined with *The Bondage Breaker* will show you how to find your freedom in Christ. Realize the power of your identity in Christ!
Paperback • 239 pp. B001
Study Guide • Paper • 153 pp. G001

The Bondage Breaker
by Neil Anderson
This best-seller combines the definitive process of breaking bondages with the *Steps to Freedom in Christ*. Read this with *Victory over the Darkness* and you will be able to resolve your personal and spiritual conflicts.
Paperback • 302 pp. B002
Study Guide • Paper • 139 pp. G002

Who I Am in Christ
by Neil Anderson
36 readings and prayers based on scriptural passages that assure us of God's love and our security and freedom in His kingdom
Paperback • 288 pp. B033

Breaking Through to Spiritual Maturity
by Neil Anderson
This is a dynamic Group Study of *Victory over the Darkness* and *The Bondage Breaker*. Complete with teaching notes for a 13-week (or 26-week) Bible study, with reproducible handouts. Ideal for Sunday School classes, Bible studies and discipleship groups.
Paperback • 151 pp. G003

Walking In Freedom
by Neil T. Anderson and Rich Miller
Filled with hope and encouragement, this inspiring devotional will help you stand firm in your freedom in Christ and build a holy shield against the enemy's attack. Don't slip back into the old ways of thinking and living.
Paperback • 205 pp. B027

Daily in Christ
by Neil and Joanne Anderson
This uplifting 365 day devotional will encourage, motivate and challenge you to live *Daily in Christ*. There's a one-page devotional and brief heartfelt prayer for each day. Celebrate and experience your freedom all year.
Paperback • 365 pp. B010

The Christ-Centered Marriage
by Neil Anderson and Charles Mylander
Husbands and wives, discover and enjoy your freedom in Christ together! Break free from old habit patterns and enjoy greater intimacy, joy and fulfillment.
Paperback • 300 pp. B023

Spiritual Protection for Your Children
by Neil Anderson and Peter and Sue VanderHook
The fascinating true story of an average middle-class American family's spiritual battle on the home front, and the lessons we can all learn about protecting our families from the enemy's attacks. Includes helpful prayers for children of various ages.
Paperback • 300 pp. B021

Freedom from Addiction
by Neil Anderson and Mike and Julia Quarles
A book like no other on true recovery! This unique Christ-centered model has helped thousands break free from alcoholism, drug addiction and other addictive behaviors. The Quarles' amazing story will encourage every reader!
Paperback • 356 pp. B019

A Way of Escape
by Neil Anderson
Talking about sex is never easy. This vital book provides real answers for sexual struggles, unwanted thoughts, compulsive habits or a painful past. Don't learn to just cope; learn how to resolve your sexual issues in Christ
Paperback • 238 pp. B014